BIRD TALK

THOMAS Y. CROWELL COMPANY   NEW YORK

BIRD TALK

BY ROMA GANS

ILLUSTRATED BY JO POLSENO

LET'S-READ-AND-FIND-OUT SCIENCE BOOKS

Editors: *DR. ROMA GANS*, Professor Emeritus of Childhood Education, Teachers College, Columbia University
DR. FRANKLYN M. BRANLEY, Chairman and Astronomer of The American Museum-Hayden Planetarium

*AVAILABLE IN SPANISH

L.C. Card 71-132298
ISBN 0-690-14592-6
       0-690-14593-4 (LB)

1   2   3   4   5   6   7   8   9   10

BIRD TALK

LET'S
READ
AND
FIND
OUT

The next chance you have, listen to the birds.

If you hear "jay, jay, jay," you know a blue jay is calling.

"Cheep, cheep, cheep" tells you an English sparrow is near.

The towhee sings "drink your tea, drink your tea," over and over.

This is bird talk.

Listen to birds in spring when they are nesting.
You may hear a male cardinal sing a loud "pretty,
pretty, pretty!" You may see it dash toward
another cardinal. It will fluff out its feathers and
chirp angrily.
This means it is protecting its nesting area.

3

No other male cardinal is allowed to come into this
nesting territory. Only one other cardinal comes
there. This is his mate. She shares his territory.

If sparrows or robins fly near, the cardinal does not
fly at them or scream. Only other cardinals must
keep out.

In this territory just one pair of cardinals has its
nest.

Why does the cardinal give its sharp call? Why does it keep other cardinals away from its territory? The cardinals will need the bugs and berries to feed their young. This territory may have food for only one nest of young cardinals.

Now when you hear the song of the cardinal in spring you will know what it means. This is the cardinal's most important call. It attracts his mate, but warns other cardinals to stay away.

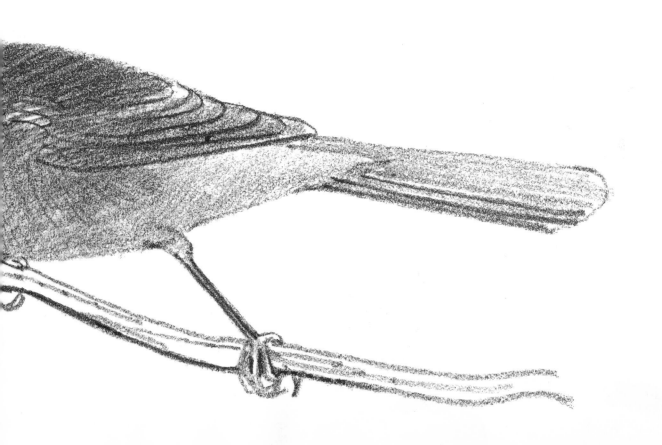

In spring a wood thrush sings early in the morning.
It sings a clear song, then flies on and stops. It
sings again, then flies on.
It flies around woods or houses and yards. The wood
thrush is claiming its nesting territory.

This means that only one pair of wood thrushes may
   build a nest here. Other kinds of birds may build a
   nest in this territory, but no other wood thrushes.
In this territory a pair of wood thrushes will find
   the bugs and berries they need to feed their young.
In nesting time many birds mark off their nesting
   territory by singing. They protect the territory
   until the young birds can fly away.

The woodpecker has no territory song. It marks off its territory by drumming with its strong beak. It drums on a dead tree, or even a tin drain pipe. Other male woodpeckers hear the noise and keep away.

Not all birds mark off territory for their nests.
Purple martins live in houses that people have built
for them. The houses have four, five, or more
"apartments." The purple martin families live side
by side and sing cheerfully. They catch gnats,
bugs, and flies in the air.

There are many gnats, bugs, and flies all around their
houses. They can find plenty of food. So purple
martins do not mark off any territory.

When we hear a bird singing it is not always singing to protect its nesting territory. Most birds have many calls and songs.

When a robin sings a song it sounds happy. When a robin makes a sharp call it sounds angry or afraid. It is giving an alarm.

As you listen carefully to birds, you will notice their
different calls.
Each kind of bird has several different calls and
songs.

We know the meaning of only some of their songs. Sometimes a wren gives an alarm cry. This means another bird is too close to the wren's nest.

The catbird cries "meow" just like a cat. This means
    it sees a cat, or a hawk, or maybe a boy nearby.
A chipping sparrow calls "s-e-e-e" to warn of danger
    when it sees a hawk. It calls "chip-chip-chip" very
    fast when it sees a cat.

The red-winged blackbird makes a "tix, tix" sound
to give an alarm. The meadow lark and other birds
stop singing as soon as they hear this alarm.

Birds tell many things by their songs and calls.

A blue jay shrieks "jay, jay, jay" when it sees a hawk. Sparrows and other small birds hide when they hear this call.

When birds sing and call, other birds hear the sound and seem to understand what is meant.

28

A mother cardinal calls softly. A young cardinal hears the call. It means "food." The young cardinal flies to be fed.

Sea gulls have a special call for other gulls when they find food.

Many birds have mating songs. The wren sings when he wants a mate. The oriole does too.

Listen to birds and watch what they do when they call or sing.

When you hear a chipping sparrow go "chip-chip-chip" see if a cat is nearby.

When you throw bread to sea gulls, see if they make
   any sounds. Do the sounds bring other sea gulls?
When you hear a clear "meow" is it a cat or a catbird?
Watch the birds and listen to them.

See if you can find out what "bird talk" is all about.

ABOUT THE AUTHOR

Roma Gans has called children "enlightened, excited citizens." She believes in the fundamental theory that children are eager to learn and will whet their own intellectual curiosity if they are encouraged by and provided with stimulating teachers and materials.

Dr. Gans received her B.S. from Columbia Teachers College and her Ph.D. from Columbia University. She began her work in the educational field in the public schools of the Middle West as a teacher, supervisor, and assistant superintendent of schools. She is Professor Emeritus of Childhood Education at Teachers College, Columbia University, and lectures extensively throughout this country and Canada.

Dr. Gans is vitally interested in nature and all its phenomena. She has many bird-feeding stations at her house in West Redding, Connecticut, where she watches birds and their habits. She enjoys living in the country, where she can observe the changing seasons of the year.

ABOUT THE ARTIST

Jo Polseno is a well-known artist who has illustrated more than one hundred text and trade books. A graduate of the University School in Bridgeport, Connecticut, and the Whitney School of Art in New Haven, he served in the U.S. Army during World War II. Until he decided to concentrate on free-lance artwork, Mr. Polseno held a variety of jobs, including a post as an instructor at the Famous Artists' School in Westport, Connecticut.

Mr. Polseno lives in Redding, Connecticut, with his wife and four children.